50
COSAS QUE NOS
ENSEÑAN LOS PERROS

50 Things Dogs Teach Us

Copyright © 2022 The Republic of Words

All rights reserved. No part of this book may be copied, reproduced, distributed, published, transmitted, broadcast, in any electronic or mechanical form, including copying or recording, without the prior written permission of the publisher.

Published by The Republic of Words
www.therepublicofwords.com
Miami, FL

© Editorial Design: 2022, Jhon Simancas

Image credits:
#1 Shutterstock Seregraff, #2 Unsplash Mitchell Luo, #3 Shutterstock Cindy Hughes, #4 Unsplash Isabel Vittrup, #5 Unsplash Linda Mynhardt, #6 Shutterstock Everett Collection, #7 Unsplash Leio Mclaren, #8 Shutterstock Schankz, #9 Shutterstock Reshetnikov_art, #10 Shutterstock Noska Photo, #11 Shutterstock Harbachova Yuliya, #12 Shuttestock. Joshua Kirk, #13 Shutterstock Lana Kray, #14 Shutterstock Diablo Gato, #15 Unsplash Charles Deluvio, #16 Unsplash James Watson, #17 #Shutterstock Judith Photo, #18 Unsplash Dasha Urvachova, #19 Shutterstock Black Lemon, #20 Unsplash Rafael Forseck, #21 Unsplash Caleb Woods, #22 Shutterstock Denisa V, #23 Shutterstock Mariano Gaspar, #24 Shutterstock Giocalde, #25 Unsplash Max Kleinen, #26 Shutterstock VirtualShutter, #27 Shutterstock Denis Moskvinov, #28 Unsplash Eve, #29 Unsplash Anthony Duran, #30 Unsplash Ja San Miguel, #31 Shutterstock Alex Zotov, #32 Shutterstock Javier Brosch, #33 Unsplash Abbey Graves, #34 Unsplash Anthony Duran, #35 Unsplash Florian Roost, #36 Unsplash Darinka Kievskaya, #37 Shutterstock Steven Bognar, #38 Shutterstock Uryupina Nadezhda, #39 Shutterstock Smrm1977, #40 Shutterstock Bazelyuk Evgeniya, #41 Unsplash Yehor Tulinov, #42 Shutterstock Eudyptula #43 Shutterstock Seregraff, #44 Unsplash Anusha Barwa, #45 Shutterstock Rita Kochmarjova, #46 Unsplash Myriam Jessier, #47 Shutterstock Javier Brosch, #48 Shutterstock RN23W, #49 Unplash Cole Wyland, #50 Shutterstock_Victor Santacruz, #51 Shutterstock Alex Zotov

Paws: Freepik.com. Decorative elements of the cover and book have been designed using images from Freepik.com.

Printed in the United States of America

50 COSAS QUE NOS ENSEÑAN LOS PERROS

MARIANELA TOLEDO

Everything I know I learned from dogs."

NORA ROBERTS
(author, The Search)

— 1 —

That there are so
many reasons
to be happy.

— 2 —

A look says it all.

— 3 —

To be brave.

— 4 —

And leave
grudges aside.

— 5 —

Although sometimes,
it is necessary to ask
for forgiveness.

— 6 —

To defend
what we love.

— 7 —

The meaning of loyalty.

— 8 —

Not to judge.

— 9 —

To trust.

— 10 —

To help.

— 11 —

To believe.

— 12 —

Age?
It's just a number.

— 13 —

To provide companionship.

— 14 —

Love at first sight.

— 15 —

To live in the present.

— 16 —

Emergencies exist.

— 17 —

To share.

— **18** —

You are important.

— 19 —

To always be ready
for an adventure.

— 20 —

To accept ourselves
as we are.

— 21 —

Race? What are you talking about?

— 22 —

To follow your instinct.

— 23 —

Impaired? What's that?

— 24 —

The end, sometimes, justifies the means.

— 25 —

Diet?
No, thank you…!

— 26 —

Patience
is an important virtue.

— 27 —

Having fun?
It can be a dirty job.

— 28 —

Water doesn't
really get you wet.

— 29 —

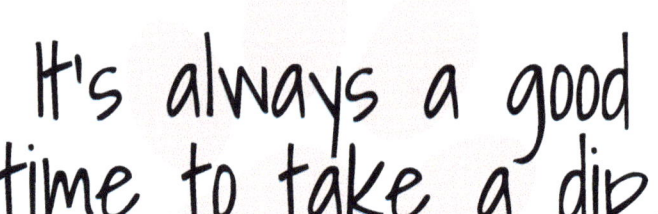

It's always a good
time to take a dip.

— 30 —

Sunny days
are beautiful...

— 31 —

And rainy days too.

— 32 —

You have to look
for treasures.

— 33 —

Having fun is
serious business.

— 34 —

Sport is, essentially, important.

— 35 —

Definition of a toy?
Everything.

— 36 —

You have to insist on what you want.

— 37 —

To be independent.

— 38 —

Almost everything can be learned.

— 39 —

The value of material things is relative.

— 40 —

To hope for the best.

– 41 –

To be alert
to intruders.

— 42 —

And to be attentive
to the command voice.

— 43 —

To be obedient.

— 44 —

A total stranger can become family.

— 45 —

There is room for everyone.

— 46 —

To not lose sight of the objective.

— 47 —

Friendship is fundamental.

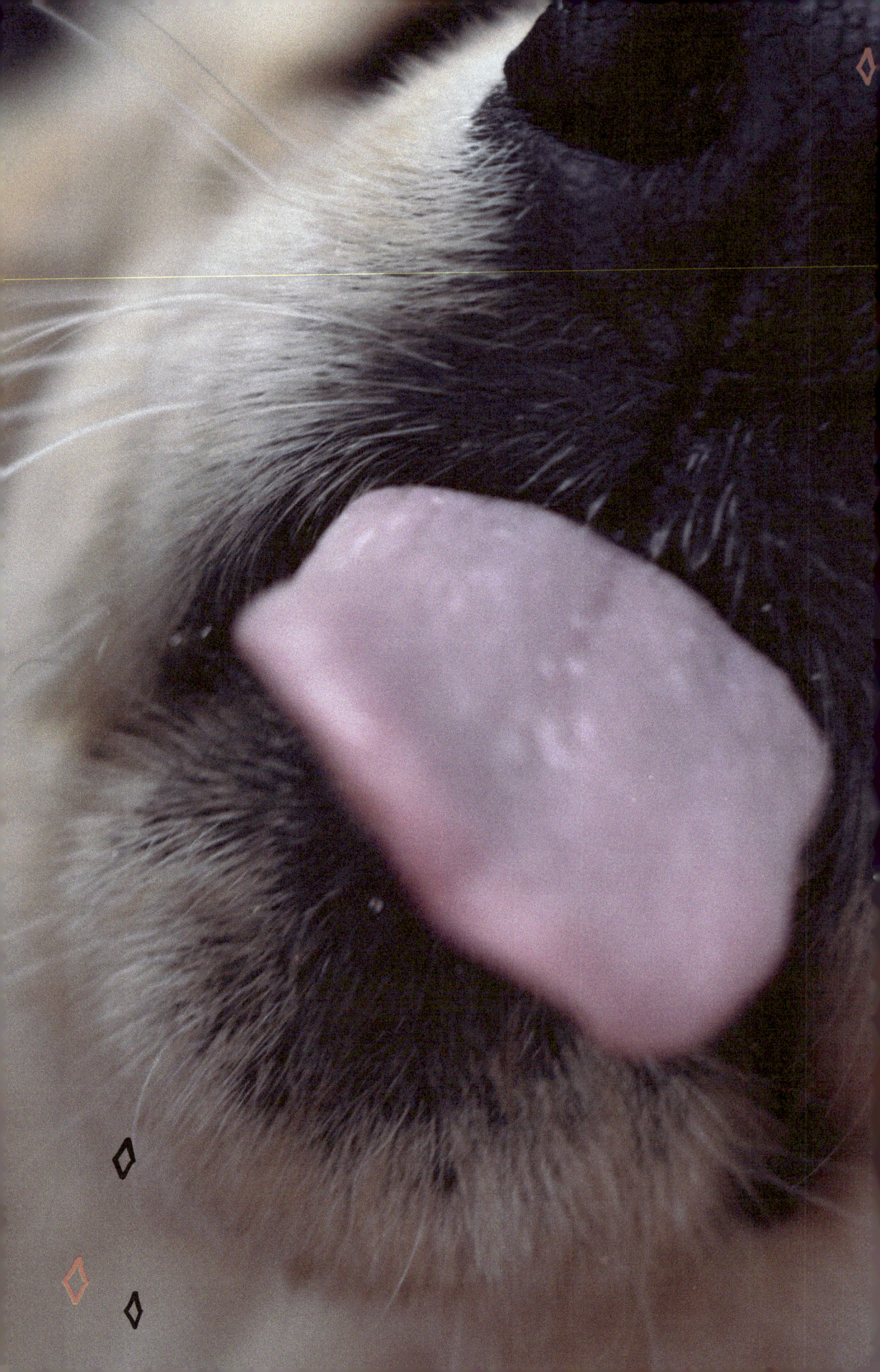

— 48 —

There is no limit to kissing.

— 49 —

To be grateful.

— 50 —

Unconditional love.

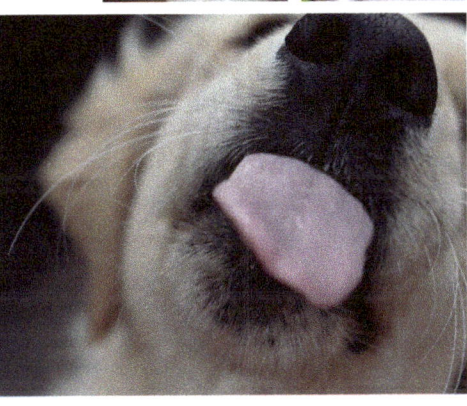

DEDICATED A JEKYLL & HYDE